all washed up

We're proud to present Drew Emborsky's latest crochet designs, a collection of all-original dishcloths using cotton yarn. Make them as gifts. Make them for yourself. But whatever you do, be sure to make them fun!

Drew Emborsky, aka The Crochet Dude®, was taught to crochet at age five by his mom while snowbound in Lake Tahoe. After studying fine art in college and doing the "starving artist" thing for years, he found solace in crocheting for charity while grieving the passing of his mom. It was during this time with the charity group that he became known as The Crochet Dude, which then led to the launch of his wildly popular blog, www.thecrochetdude.com. Since then, Drew has published numerous patterns in magazines and compilation books, his own full-length books, appeared as a guest on various TV programs, and is currently the crochet expert on the hit PBS show "Knit and Crochet Today." Drew lives in Houston, Texas with his cats Chandler and Cleocatra.

LEISURE ARTS, INC.
Little Rock, Arkansas

#1 Tackle It with a Twist!
Shown on Front Cover.
Finished Size: 10"w x 8"h
(25.5 cm x 20.5 cm)

 EASY

MATERIALS

Medium Weight Yarn MEDIUM 4

[3.5 ounces, 207 yards
(100 grams, 188 meters) per skein]: 1 skein
Crochet hook, size I (5.5 mm) **or** size needed for gauge

GAUGE SWATCH: 3¹/₂"w x 2³/₄"h (9 cm x 7 cm)
Ch 12.
Work same as Dishcloth for 7 rows.
Finish off.

DISHCLOTH
Ch 32.

Row 1: Sc in second ch from hook and in each ch across: 31 sc.

To work Bobble (uses one sc), insert hook in sc indicated, YO and pull up a loop (2 loops on hook), (YO and draw through one loop on hook) 4 times (ch 4 made), YO and draw through both loops on hook.

Row 2 (Right side)**:** Ch 1, turn; sc in first sc, (work Bobble in next sc, sc in next sc) across: 16 sc and 15 Bobbles.

Row 3: Ch 1, turn; sc in each st across.

Rows 4 and 5: Repeat Rows 2 and 3.

Row 6: Ch 4 (**counts as first dc plus ch 1**), turn; skip next sc, dc in next sc, ★ ch 1, skip next sc, dc in next sc; repeat from ★ across: 16 dc and 15 ch-1 sps.

Row 7: Ch 1, turn; sc in first dc and in each ch-1 sp and each dc across: 31 sc.

Rows 8-23: Repeat Rows 2-7 twice, then repeat Rows 2-5 once **more.**

Finish off.

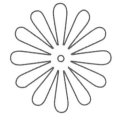

#2 Extra Elbow Grease!
Shown on Front Cover.
Finished Size: 4¹/₂" (11.5 cm) diameter

EASY

MATERIALS

Medium Weight Yarn **4** MEDIUM
[3.5 ounces, 207 yards
(100 grams, 188 meters) per skein]: 1 skein
Crochet hook, size I (5.5 mm) **or** size needed for gauge
Yarn needle

GAUGE SWATCH: 2" (5 cm) square
Ch 8.
Row 1: Sc in second ch from hook and in each ch across: 7 sc.
Rows 2-7: Ch 1, turn; sc in each sc across.
Finish off.

DISHCLOTH

Leaving a long end for sewing, ch 20; being careful not to twist ch, join with slip st to form a ring.

Rnd 1 (Right side): Ch 1, sc in same ch as joining, ch 2, (sc in next ch, ch 2) around; do **not** join, place a marker to mark the beginning of the rnd *(see Markers, page 29)*: 20 sc and 20 ch-2 sps.

Rnds 2-14: (Sc in next sc, ch 2) around; at end of Rnd 14, slip st in next sc to join and finish off leaving a long end for sewing.

Thread yarn needle with long end and weave through sc on Rnd 14; gather **tightly** and secure end.

Thread yarn needle with long end of beginning ch. Weave through each ch of beginning ch; gather **tightly** and secure end.

#3 Grime Buster!

Shown on Front Cover.
Finished Size: 10"w x 9¹/₂"h
(25.5 cm x 24 cm)

◖◼▢▢▷ EASY

MATERIALS

Medium Weight Yarn
[3.5 ounces, 207 yards
(100 grams, 188 meters) per skein]:
MC (Green) - 1 skein
Color A (Blue) - 1 skein
Color B (White) - 1 skein
Crochet hook, size I (5.5 mm) **or** size needed for gauge

GAUGE SWATCH: 2"w x 2¹/₄"h (5 cm x 5.75 cm)
With MC, ch 9.
Work same as Center for 4 rows.
Finish off.

CENTER
With MC, ch 29; place a marker in third ch from hook
for Border placement.

Row 1: Dc in fourth ch from hook **(3 skipped chs count as first dc)** and in each ch across: 27 dc.

To work Back Post double crochet (abbreviated BPdc), YO, insert hook from **back** to **front** around post of st indicated *(Fig. 3, page 30)*, YO and pull up a loop (3 loops on hook), (YO and draw through 2 loops on hook) twice.

> *To work Front Post double crochet* (abbreviated *FPdc)*, YO, insert hook from **front** to **back** around post of st indicated *(Fig. 3, page 30)*, YO and pull up a loop (3 loops on hook), (YO and draw through 2 loops on hook) twice.

Row 2 (Right side)**:** Ch 2 (**counts as first hdc, now and throughout**), turn; work FPdc around next dc, (work BPdc around next dc, work FPdc around next dc) across to last dc, hdc in last dc; finish off.

Note: Loop a short piece of yarn around any stitch to mark Row 2 as **right** side.

Row 3: With **wrong** side facing, join Color A with hdc in first hdc *(see Joining With Hdc, page 29)*; work FPdc around next st, (work BPdc around next st, work FPdc around next st) across to last hdc, hdc in last hdc.

Row 4: Ch 2, turn; work FPdc around next st, (work BPdc around next st, work FPdc around next st) across to last hdc, hdc in last hdc; finish off.

Rows 5 and 6: With Color B, repeat Rows 3 and 4.

Rows 7 and 8: With MC, repeat Rows 3 and 4.

Rows 9-14: Repeat Rows 3-8; at end of Row 14, do **not** finish off.

Instructions continued on page 8.

BORDER

Rnd 1: Ch 1, do **not** turn; work 23 sc evenly spaced across end of rows; (sc, ch 1, sc) in marked ch (corner made), sc in free loop of next 25 chs *(Fig. 1, page 30)*, (sc, ch 1, sc) in last ch (corner made); work 23 sc evenly spaced across end of rows; (sc, ch 1, sc) in first hdc of Row 14 (corner made), sc in next 25 sts, (sc, ch 1, sc) in last hdc (corner made); join with slip st to first sc, finish off: 104 sc and 4 corner ch-1 sps.

Rnd 2: With **right** side facing, join Color A with sc in any corner ch-1 sp *(see Joining With Sc, page 29)*; ch 1, sc in same sp, ★ sc in Back Loop Only *(Fig. 2, page 30)* of each sc across to next corner ch-1 sp, (sc, ch 1, sc) in corner sp; repeat from ★ 2 times **more**, sc in Back Loop Only of each sc across; join with slip st to **both** loops of first sc, finish off: 112 sc and 4 corner ch-1 sps.

Rnd 3: With Color B, repeat Rnd 2: 120 sc and 4 corner ch-1 sps.

Rnd 4: With **right** side facing, join MC with sc in any corner ch-1 sp; [ch 1, sc in top of sc just made *(Fig. A, Picot made)]*, skip next sc, ★ (sc in Back Loop Only of next sc, work Picot, skip next sc) across to next corner ch-1 sp, sc in corner sp, work Picot, skip next sc; repeat from ★ 2 times **more**, (sc in Back Loop Only of next sc, work Picot, skip next sc) across; join with slip st to first sc, finish off.

Fig. A

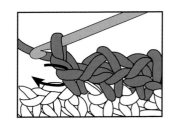

#4 Lots of Suds!

Shown on Front Cover.

Finished Size: 10³/₄"w x 9³/₄"h

(27.5 cm x 25 cm)

◖■◼□▭ EASY

MATERIALS

Medium Weight Yarn
[3.5 ounces, 207 yards
(100 grams, 188 meters) per skein]:
MC (Green) - 1 skein
CC (White) - 1 skein
Crochet hook, size I (5.5 mm) **or** size needed for gauge

GAUGE SWATCH: 3" (7.5 cm) square
Ch 14.
Work same as Center for 5 rows.
Finish off.

CENTER

With MC, ch 36; place a marker in fourth ch from hook for Border placement.

Row 1 (Right side)**:** Dc in sixth ch from hook
(5 skipped chs count as first dc plus ch 1 and 1 skipped ch), place marker around dc just made for Ruffle placement, ★ ch 1, skip next ch, dc in next ch; repeat from ★ across: 17 dc and 16 ch-1 sps.

Note: Loop a short piece of yarn around any stitch to mark Row 1 as **right** side.

Instructions continued on page 10.

Rows 2-12: Ch 4 **(counts as first dc plus ch 1)**, turn; dc in next dc, (ch 1, dc in next dc) across; at end of Row 12, do **not** finish off.

BORDER

Rnd 1: Ch 1, turn; (sc, ch 1, sc) in first dc (corner made), sc in next ch-1 sp and in each dc and ch-1 sp across to last dc, (sc, ch 1, sc) in last dc (corner made); working in end of rows, sc in first row, 2 sc in each of next 11 rows; working in free loops *(Fig. 1, page 30)* and in sps across beginning ch, (sc, ch 1, sc) in first ch, sc in next ch-1 sp, (sc in next ch, sc in next ch-1 sp) across to marked ch, (sc, ch 1, sc) in marked ch; working in end of rows, 2 sc in each of first 11 rows, sc in last row; join with slip st to first sc: 116 sc and 4 corner ch-1 sps.

Rnd 2: Ch 3 **(counts as first dc)**, (2 dc, ch 2, 2 dc) in next corner ch-1 sp, ★ dc in next sc and in each sc across to next corner ch-1 sp, (2 dc, ch 2, 2 dc) in corner sp; repeat from ★ 2 times **more**, dc in next sc and in each sc across; join with slip st to first dc: 132 dc and 4 corner ch-2 sps.

Rnd 3: Ch 1, sc in same st as joining, [ch 1, sc in top of sc just made *(Fig. B,* **Picot made**)], skip next dc, sc in next dc, work Picot, sc in next corner ch-2 sp, work Picot, ★ sc in next dc, work Picot, (skip next dc, sc in next dc, work Picot) across to next corner ch-2 sp, sc in corner sp, work Picot; repeat from ★ 2 times **more**, (sc in next dc, work Picot, skip next dc) across; join with slip st to first sc, finish off.

Fig. B

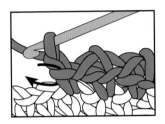

RUFFLE
Ruffle is worked around post of dc on Center, inserting hook from front to back around each st *(Fig. 3, page 30).*

With **right** side facing, join CC with sc around second dc on Row 12 *(see Joining With Sc, page 29)*; ★ † (ch 5, sc around next dc) 14 times, ch 5, turn Dishcloth 180° clockwise, sc around second dc on next row, (ch 5, sc around next dc) 14 times †, ch 5, **turn** Dishcloth 180° counterclockwise, sc around second dc on next row; repeat from ★ 4 times **more**, then repeat from † to † once; finish off.

#5 Put Your Heart into It!
Shown on page 12.
Finished Size: 9³/₄" (25 cm) square

 EASY

MATERIALS
Medium Weight Yarn
[3.5 ounces, 207 yards
(100 grams, 188 meters) per skein]: 1 skein
Crochet hook, size I (5.5 mm) **or** size needed for gauge

GAUGE: 14 sc and 14 rows = 4" (10 cm)

Gauge Swatch: 2" (5 cm) square
Ch 8.
Row 1: Sc in second ch from hook and in each ch
across: 7 sc.
Rows 2-7: Ch 1, turn; sc in each sc across.
Finish off.

CENTER
Ch 23.

Row 1: Sc in second ch from hook and in each ch across:
22 sc.

To work Bobble (uses one sc), insert hook in sc
indicated, YO and pull up a loop (2 loops on hook),
(YO and draw through one loop on hook) 4 times
(ch 4 made), YO and draw through both loops on hook.

Row 2 (Right side)**:** Ch 1, turn; sc in first 5 sc, work Bobble
in next sc, sc in next 10 sc, work Bobble in next sc, sc in
last 5 sc: 20 sc and 2 Bobbles.

Instructions continued on page 14.

Row 3: Ch 1, turn; sc in each st across: 22 sc.

Row 4: Ch 1, turn; sc in first 4 sc, work Bobble in next sc, sc in next sc, work Bobble in next sc, sc in next 8 sc, work Bobble in next sc, sc in next sc, work Bobble in next sc, sc in last 4 sc: 18 sc and 4 Bobbles.

Row 5: Ch 1, turn; sc in each st across: 22 sc.

Row 6: Ch 1, turn; sc in first 3 sc, work Bobble in next sc, sc in next 3 sc, work Bobble in next sc, sc in next 6 sc, (work Bobble in next sc, sc in next 3 sc) twice: 18 sc and 4 Bobbles.

Row 7: Ch 1, turn; sc in each st across: 22 sc.

Row 8: Ch 1, turn; sc in first 2 sc, work Bobble in next sc, sc in next 5 sc, work Bobble in next sc, sc in next 4 sc, work Bobble in next sc, sc in next 5 sc, work Bobble in next sc, sc in last 2 sc: 18 sc and 4 Bobbles.

Row 9: Ch 1, turn; sc in each st across: 22 sc.

Row 10: Ch 1, turn; sc in first 2 sc, work Bobble in next sc, (sc in next 2 sc, work Bobble in next sc) twice, sc in next 4 sc, (work Bobble in next sc, sc in next 2 sc) 3 times: 16 sc and 6 Bobbles.

Row 11: Ch 1, turn; sc in each st across: 22 sc.

Row 12: Ch 1, turn; sc in first 3 sc, work Bobble in next sc, sc in next 3 sc, work Bobble in next sc, sc in next 6 sc, (work Bobble in next sc, sc in next 3 sc) twice: 18 sc and 4 Bobbles.

Row 13: Ch 1, turn; sc in each st across: 22 sc.

Rows 14-25: Repeat Rows 2-13; at end of Row 25, do **not** finish off.

BORDER

Rnd 1: Ch 1, turn; sc in each sc across, ch 2 (corner sp made); work 22 sc evenly spaced across end of rows, ch 2 (corner sp made); working in free loops of beginning ch *(Fig. 1, page 30)*, sc in ch at base of first sc and in each ch across, ch 2 (corner sp made); work 22 sc evenly spaced across end of rows, ch 2 (corner sp made); join with slip st to first sc: 88 sc and 4 corner ch-2 sps.

Rnd 2: Ch 1, do **not** turn; sc in same st as joining, ★ † ch 2, skip next sc, (sc in next sc, ch 2, skip next sc) across to next corner ch-2 sp, (sc, ch 2) twice in corner sp †, sc in next sc; repeat from ★ 2 times **more**, then repeat from † to † once; join with slip st to first sc: 52 ch-2 sps.

Rnd 3: (Slip st, ch 1, sc) in next ch-1 sp, ch 3, (sc in next ch-2 sp, ch 3) 10 times, (sc, ch 3) twice in next ch-2 sp, ★ (sc in next ch-2 sp, ch 3) 12 times, (sc, ch 3) twice in next ch-2 sp; repeat from ★ 2 times **more**, sc in last ch-2 sp, ch 3; join with slip st to first sc: 56 ch-3 sps.

Rnd 4: Slip st in next ch-3 sp, ch 1, 3 sc in same sp and in each of next 10 ch-3 sps, 5 sc in next ch-3 sp, (3 sc in each of next 13 ch-3 sps, 5 sc in next ch-3 sp) 3 times, 3 sc in each of last 2 ch-3 sps; join with slip st to first sc: 176 sc.

Rnd 5: Ch 1, sc in same st as joining, ch 2, (sc in next sc, ch 2) around; join with slip st to first sc, finish off.

#6 Real Men Do Dishes!
Shown on page 12.
Finished Size: 9" (23 cm) square

 EASY

MATERIALS
Medium Weight Yarn ![MEDIUM 4]
[3.5 ounces, 207 yards
(100 grams, 188 meters) per skein]: 1 skein
Crochet hook, size I (5.5 mm) **or** size needed for gauge

GAUGE SWATCH: 2½"w x 2¼"h (6.25 cm x 5.75 cm)
Ch 10.
Work same as Dishcloth for 5 rows.
Finish off.

DISHCLOTH
Ch 34.

Row 1: Sc in second ch from hook and in each ch across: 33 sc.

Row 2 (Right side): Ch 3 **(counts as first dc)**, turn; dc in next sc and in each sc across.

To work Back Post double crochet (abbreviated BPdc), YO, insert hook from **back** to **front** around post of st indicated *(Fig. 3, page 30)*, YO and pull up a loop (3 loops on hook), (YO and draw through 2 loops on hook) twice.

To work Front Post double crochet (abbreviated FPdc), YO, insert hook from **front** to **back** around post of st indicated *(Fig. 3, page 30)*, YO and pull up a loop (3 loops on hook), (YO and draw through 2 loops on hook) twice.

Row 3: Ch 2 **(counts as first hdc, now and throughout)**, turn; work BPdc around next dc, (work FPdc around next dc, work BPdc around next dc) across to last dc, hdc in last dc.

To work Front Post treble crochet (abbreviated FPtr), YO twice, insert hook from **front** to **back** around post of st indicated *(Fig. 3, page 30)*, YO and pull up a loop (4 loops on hook), (YO and draw through 2 loops on hook) 3 times.

Row 4: Ch 2, turn; skip next 2 sts, work FPtr around next st, working **behind** FPtr just made, work BPdc around second skipped st, working in **front** of last 2 sts made, work FPtr around first skipped st, ★ work BPdc around next st, skip next 2 sts, work FPtr around next st, working **behind** FPtr just made, work BPdc around second skipped st, working in **front** of last 2 sts made, work FPtr around first skipped st; repeat from ★ across to last hdc, hdc in last hdc.

Row 5: Ch 2, turn; work BPdc around next st, (work FPdc around next st, work BPdc around next st) across to last hdc, hdc in last hdc.

Rows 6-20: Repeat Rows 4 and 5, 7 times; then repeat Row 4 once **more**.

Row 21: Ch 1, turn; sc in each st across; finish off.

#7 Finished with a Flourish!
Shown on Back Cover.
Finished Size: 10¹/₄"w x 10"h
(26 cm x 25.5 cm)

◧■◨☐◨ **EASY**

MATERIALS
Medium Weight Yarn
[3.5 ounces, 207 yards
(100 grams, 188 meters) per skein]: 1 skein
Crochet hook, size I (5.5 mm) **or** size needed for gauge

GAUGE SWATCH: 2³/₄" (7 cm) square
Ch 12.
Work same as Center for 10 rows.
Finish off.

CENTER
Ch 32.

Row 1 (Right side): Sc in second ch from hook, ★ ch 1, skip next ch, sc in next ch; repeat from ★ across: 16 sc and 15 ch-1 sps.

Row 2: Ch 1, turn; sc in first sc and in next ch-1 sp, ch 1, (sc in next ch-1 sp, ch 1) across to last ch-1 sp, sc in last ch-1 sp and in last sc: 17 sc and 14 ch-1 sps.

Row 3: Ch 1, turn; sc in first sc, ch 1, (sc in next ch-1 sp, ch 1) across to last 2 sc, skip next sc, sc in last sc: 16 sc and 15 ch-1 sps.

Rows 4-31: Repeat Rows 2 and 3, 14 times; at end of Row 31, do **not** finish off.

BORDER

Rnd 1: Ch 1, do **not** turn; working in end of rows, (sc, ch 2, sc) in Row 31, ch 1, skip next row, (sc in next row, ch 1, skip next row) 14 times, (sc, ch 2, sc) in Row 1, ch 1; working in sps across beginning ch, (sc in next sp, ch 1) 15 times; working in end of rows, (sc, ch 2, sc) in Row 1, ch 1, skip next row, (sc in next row, ch 1, skip next row) 14 times, (sc, ch 2, sc) in Row 31, ch 1; working in ch-1 sps across Row 31, (sc in next ch-1 sp, ch 1) 15 times; join with slip st to first sc: 66 sps.

Rnd 2: Slip st in next corner ch-2 sp, ch 1, (sc, ch 2, sc) in same corner sp, † ch 1, (sc in next ch-1 sp, ch 1) 15 times, (sc, ch 2, sc) in next corner ch-2 sp, ch 1, (sc in next ch-1 sp, ch 1) 16 times †, (sc, ch 2, sc) in next corner ch-2 sp, repeat from † to † once; join with slip st to first sc: 70 sps.

Rnd 3: Slip st in next corner ch-2 sp, ch 3 **(counts as first dc)**, 2 dc in same corner sp, † dc in next ch-1 sp, working **around** dc just made, dc in previous corner sp, (dc in next sp, working **around** dc just made, dc in previous sp) 16 times, 3 dc in same corner sp, dc in next ch-1 sp, working **around** dc just made, dc in previous corner sp, (dc in next sp, working **around** dc just made, dc in previous sp) 17 times †, 3 dc in same corner sp, repeat from † to † once; join with slip st to first dc: 152 dc.

Rnd 4: Ch 1, sc in same st as joining, ch 1, (sc in next dc, ch 1) 3 times, † skip next dc, (sc in next dc, ch 1, skip next dc) 16 times, (sc in next dc, ch 1) 4 times, skip next dc, (sc in next dc, ch 1, skip next dc) 17 times †, (sc in next dc, ch 1) 4 times, repeat from † to † once; join with slip st to first sc, finish off.

#8 Nine Rounds and You're Done!
Shown on Back Cover.
Finished Size: 9" (23 cm) diameter

 EASY

MATERIALS
Medium Weight Yarn
[3.5 ounces, 207 yards
(100 grams, 188 meters) per skein]:
Color A (Off-White) - 1 skein
Color B (Brown) - 1 skein
Color C (Lt Gold) - 1 skein
Crochet hook, size I (5.5 mm) **or** size needed for gauge

GAUGE SWATCH: 3" (7.5 cm) diameter
Work same as Dishcloth for 3 rnds.

DISHCLOTH
Rnd 1 (Right side)**:** With Color A, ch 4, 11 dc in fourth ch from hook (**3 skipped chs count as first dc**); join with slip st to first dc, finish off: 12 dc.

Note: Loop a short piece of yarn around any stitch to mark Rnd 1 as **right** side.

To work Back Post double crochet (abbreviated *BPdc)*, YO, insert hook from **back** to **front** around post of st indicated *(Fig. 3, page 30)*, YO and pull up a loop (3 loops on hook), (YO and draw through 2 loops on hook) twice.

To work Front Post double crochet (abbreviated *FPdc)*, YO, insert hook from **front** to **back** around post of st indicated *(Fig. 3, page 30)*, YO and pull up a loop (3 loops on hook), (YO and draw through 2 loops on hook) twice.

Rnd 2: With **right** side facing, join Color B with dc from **back** to **front** around post of same st as joining *(see Joining With Dc, page 29 and Fig. 3, page 30)* (first BPdc made); ch 1, work FPdc around next dc, ch 1, ★ work BPdc around next dc, ch 1, work FPdc around next dc, ch 1; repeat from ★ around; join with slip st to first BPdc: 12 sts and 12 ch-1 sps.

Rnd 3: Slip st in next ch-1 sp, ch 3 **(counts as first dc)**, work FPdc around next FPdc, dc in next ch-1 sp, work BPdc around next BPdc, ★ dc in next ch-1 sp, work FPdc around next FPdc, dc in next ch-1 sp, work BPdc around next BPdc; repeat from ★ around; join with slip st to first dc, finish off: 24 sts.

Instructions continued on page 22.

Rnd 4: With **right** side facing, join Color A with dc in same st as joining; ch 2, dc in same st, work FPdc around next FPdc, (dc, ch 2, dc) in next dc, work BPdc around next BPdc, ★ (dc, ch 2, dc) in next dc, work FPdc around next FPdc, (dc, ch 2, dc) in next dc, work BPdc around next BPdc; repeat from ★ around; join with slip st to first dc, finish off: 36 sts and 12 ch-2 sps.

Rnd 5: With **right** side facing, join Color C with dc in ch-2 sp after joining st; ch 2, 2 dc in same sp, skip next dc, work FPdc around next FPdc, (2 dc, ch 2, 2 dc) in next ch-2 sp, skip next dc, work BPdc around next BPdc, ★ (2 dc, ch 2, 2 dc) in next ch-2 sp, skip next dc, work FPdc around next FPdc, (2 dc, ch 2, 2 dc) in next ch-2 sp, skip next dc, work BPdc around next BPdc; repeat from ★ around, dc in same sp as first dc; join with slip st to first dc: 60 sts and 12 ch-2 sps.

Rnd 6: Slip st in next ch-2 sp, ch 5 **(counts as first dc plus ch 2)**, dc in same sp, work FPdc around each of next 5 sts, (dc, ch 2, dc) in next ch-2 sp, work FPdc around each of next 2 dc, work BPdc around next BPdc, work FPdc around each of next 2 dc, ★ (dc, ch 2, dc) in next ch-2 sp, work FPdc around each of next 5 sts, (dc, ch 2, dc) in next ch-2 sp, work FPdc around each of next 2 dc, work BPdc around next BPdc, work FPdc around each of next 2 dc; repeat from ★ around; join with slip st to first dc, finish off: 84 sts and 12 ch-2 sps.

Rnd 7: With **right** side facing, join Color A with dc in ch-2 sp after joining st; 4 dc in same sp, skip next dc, work FPdc around each of next 5 FPdc, 5 dc in next ch-2 sp, skip next dc, work FPdc around each of next 2 FPdc, work BPdc around next BPdc, work FPdc around each of next 2 FPdc, ★ 5 dc in next ch-2 sp, skip next dc, work FPdc around each of next 5 FPdc, 5 dc in next ch-2 sp, skip next dc, work FPdc around each of next 2 FPdc, work BPdc around next BPdc, work FPdc around each of next 2 FPdc; repeat from ★ around; join with slip st to first dc, finish off: 120 sts.

Rnd 8: With **right** side facing and working in Back Loops Only *(Fig. 2, page 30)*, join Color B with dc in any st; dc in next st and in each st around; join with slip st to **both** loops of first dc.

Rnd 9: Ch 1, working in both loops, sc in same st as joining, ch 1, (sc in next dc, ch 1) around; join with slip st to first sc, finish off.

#9 One Red-Hot Scrubber!
Shown on Back Cover.
Finished Size: 10¹/₂" (26.5 cm) square

◧■□◻ **EASY**

MATERIALS
Medium Weight Yarn  **4** MEDIUM
[3.5 ounces, 207 yards
(100 grams, 188 meters) per skein]:
MC (Dk Pink) - 1 skein
Color A (Off-White) - 1 skein
Color B (Lt Gold) - 1 skein
Crochet hook, size I (5.5 mm) **or** size needed for gauge

GAUGE SWATCH: 2⁷/₈"w x 2"h (7.25 cm x 5 cm)
With MC, ch 11.
Work same as Center for 4 rows.
Finish off.

CENTER
With MC, ch 27.

Row 1: Sc in second ch from hook and in each
ch across: 26 sc.

> ***To work treble crochet*** *(abbreviated tr)*, YO twice,
> insert hook in st indicated, YO and pull up a loop
> (4 loops on hook), (YO and draw through 2 loops on
> hook) 3 times.

Row 2 (Right side): Ch 3 **(counts as first dc, now and throughout)**, turn; ★ skip next sc, dc in next 3 sc, working in **front** of 3 dc just made, tr in skipped sc; repeat from ★ across to last sc, dc in last sc: 20 dc and 6 tr.

Note: Loop a short piece of yarn around any stitch to mark Row 2 as **right** side.

Row 3: Ch 3, turn; ★ skip next tr, dc in next 3 dc, working **behind** 3 dc just made, tr in skipped tr; repeat from ★ across to last dc, dc in last dc.

Row 4: Ch 3, turn; ★ skip next tr, dc in next 3 dc, working in **front** of 3 dc just made, tr in skipped tr; repeat from ★ across to last dc, dc in last dc.

Rows 5-13: Repeat Rows 3 and 4, 4 times; then repeat Row 3 once **more**; at end of Row 13, do **not** finish off.

BORDER

Rnd 1: Ch 1, turn; (sc, ch 1, sc) in first dc (corner made), sc in next 24 sts, (sc, ch 1, sc) in last dc (corner made); work 24 sc evenly spaced across end of rows; working in free loops of beginning ch *(Fig. 1, page 30)*, (sc, ch 1, sc) in ch at base of first sc (corner made), sc in next 24 chs, (sc, ch 1, sc) in last ch (corner made); work 24 sc evenly spaced across end of rows; join with slip st to first sc, finish off: 104 sc and 4 corner ch-1 sps.

Instructions continued on page 26.

Rnd 2: With **right** side facing, join Color A with sc in any corner ch-1 sp *(see Joining With Sc, page 29)*; ch 1, sc in same sp, ★ sc in Back Loop Only *(Fig. 2, page 30)* of next sc and each sc across to next corner ch-1 sp, (sc, ch 1, sc) in corner sp; repeat from ★ 2 times **more**, sc in Back Loop Only of next sc and each sc across; join with slip st to **both** loops of first sc, finish off: 112 sc and 4 corner ch-1 sps.

Rnd 3: With **right** side facing, join Color B with dc in any corner ch-1 sp *(see Joining With Dc, page 29)*; (dc, ch 2, 2 dc) in same sp, ★ dc in Back Loop Only of next sc and each sc across to next corner ch-1 sp, (2 dc, ch 2, 2 dc) in corner sp; repeat from ★ 2 times **more**, dc in Back Loop Only of next sc and each sc across; join with slip st to **both** loops of first dc, finish off: 128 dc and 4 corner ch-2 sps.

Rnd 4: With **right** side facing, join Color A with sc in any corner ch-2 sp; ch 1, sc in same sp, ★ sc in Back Loop Only of next dc and each dc across to next corner ch-2 sp, (sc, ch 1, sc) in corner sp; repeat from ★ 2 times **more**, sc in Back Loop Only of next dc and each dc across; join with slip st to **both** loops of first sc, finish off: 136 sc and 4 corner ch-1 sps.

Rnd 5: With **right** side facing, join MC with slip st in any corner ch-1 sp; ch 1, working from **left** to **right**, work reverse sc *(Figs. 4a-d, page 31)* in Back Loop Only of each sc and in each corner ch-1 sp around; join with slip st to **both** loops of first st, finish off.

GENERAL INSTRUCTIONS

ABBREVIATIONS

BPdc	Back Post double crochet(s)
CC	Contrasting Color
ch(s)	chain(s)
cm	centimeters
dc	double crochet(s)
FPdc	Front Post double crochet(s)
FPtr	Front Post treble crochet(s)
hdc	half double crochet(s)
MC	Main Color
mm	millimeters
Rnd(s)	Round(s)
sc	single crochet(s)
sp(s)	space(s)
st(s)	stitch(es)
tr	treble crochet(s)
YO	yarn over

★ — work instructions following ★ as many **more** times as indicated in addition to the first time.

† to † — work all instructions from first † to second † as **many** times as specified.

( ) or [ ] — work enclosed instructions **as many** times as specified by the number immediately following **or** work all enclosed instructions in the stitch or space indicated **or** contains explanatory remarks.

colon (:) — the number(s) given after a colon at the end of a row or round denote(s) the number of stitches or spaces you should have on that row or round.

CROCHET TERMINOLOGY	
UNITED STATES	INTERNATIONAL
slip stitch (slip st) =	single crochet (sc)
single crochet (sc) =	double crochet (dc)
half double crochet (hdc) =	half treble crochet (htr)
double crochet (dc) =	treble crochet(tr)
treble crochet (tr) =	double treble crochet (dtr)
double treble crochet (dtr) =	triple treble crochet (ttr)
triple treble crochet (tr tr) =	quadruple treble crochet (qtr)
skip =	miss

CROCHET HOOKS	
Metric mm	**U.S.**
2.25	B-1
2.75	C-2
3.25	D-3
3.5	E-4
3.75	F-5
4	G-6
5	H-8
5.5	I-9
6	J-10
6.5	K-10½
9	N
10	P
15	Q

▮☐☐☐ **BEGINNER**	Projects for first-time crocheters using basic stitches. Minimal shaping.
▮▮☐☐ **EASY**	Projects using yarn with basic stitches, repetitive stitch patterns, simple color changes, and simple shaping and finishing.
▮▮▮☐ **INTERMEDIATE**	Projects using a variety of techniques, such as basic lace patterns or color patterns, mid-level shaping and finishing.
▮▮▮▮ **EXPERIENCED**	Projects with intricate stitch patterns, techniques and dimension, such as non-repeating patterns, multi-color techniques, fine threads, small hooks, detailed shaping and refined finishing.

Yarn Weight Symbol & Names	LACE 0	SUPER FINE 1	FINE 2	LIGHT 3	MEDIUM 4	BULKY 5	SUPER BULKY 6
Type of Yarns in Category	Fingering, 10-count crochet thread	Sock, Fingering Baby	Sport, Baby	DK, Light Worsted	Worsted, Afghan, Aran	Chunky, Craft, Rug	Bulky, Roving
Crochet Gauge* Ranges in Single Crochet to 4" (10 cm)	32-42 double crochets**	21-32 sts	16-20 sts	12-17 sts	11-14 sts	8-11 sts	5-9 sts
Advised Hook Size Range	Steel*** 6,7,8 Regular hook B-1	B-1 to E-4	E-4 to 7	7 to I-9	I-9 to K-10.5	K-10.5 to M-13	M-13 and larger

*GUIDELINES ONLY: The chart above reflects the most commonly used gauges and hook sizes for specific yarn categories.

** Lace weight yarns are usually crocheted on larger-size hooks to create lacy openwork patterns. Accordingly, a gauge range is difficult to determine. Always follow the gauge stated in your pattern.

*** Steel crochet hooks are sized differently from regular hooks–the higher the number the smaller the hook, which is the reverse of regular hook sizing.

GAUGE

Exact gauge is essential for proper size. Before beginning your piece, make the sample swatch given in the individual instructions in the yarn and hook specified. After completing the swatch, measure it, counting your stitches and rows or rounds carefully. If your swatch is larger or smaller than specified, **make another, changing hook size to get the correct gauge**. Keep trying until you find the size hook that will give you the specified gauge.

MARKERS

Markers are used to help distinguish the beginning of each round being worked. Place a 2" (5 cm) scrap piece of yarn before the first stitch of each round, moving the marker after each round is complete.

JOINING WITH SC

When instructed to join with a sc, begin with a slip knot on the hook. Insert the hook in or around the stitch or in the space indicated, YO and pull up a loop, YO and draw through both loops on the hook.

JOINING WITH HDC

When instructed to join with a hdc, begin with a slip knot on hook. YO, holding loop on hook, insert hook in stitch or space indicated, YO and pull up a loop, YO and draw through all 3 loops on hook.

JOINING WITH DC

When instructed to join with a dc, begin with a slip knot on hook. YO, holding loop on hook, insert the hook in or around the stitch or in the space indicated, YO and pull up a loop (3 loops on hook), (YO and draw through 2 loops on hook) twice.

FREE LOOPS OF A CHAIN

When instructed to work in free loops of a chain, work in loop indicated by arrow *(Fig. 1)*.

Fig. 1

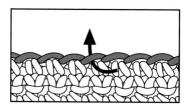

BACK LOOP ONLY

Work only in loop(s) indicated by arrow *(Fig. 2)*.

Fig. 2

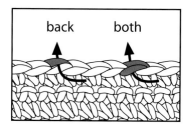

POST STITCH

Work around post of stitch indicated, inserting hook in direction of arrow *(Fig. 3)*.

Fig. 3

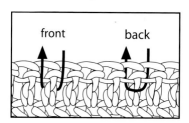

REVERSE SINGLE CROCHET

Working from **left** to **right**, ★ insert hook in stitch to right of hook *(Fig. 4a)*, YO and draw through, under and to left of loop on hook (2 loops on hook) *(Fig. 4b)*, YO and draw through both loops on hook *(Fig. 4c)* **(reverse sc made,** *Fig. 4d)*; repeat from ★ around.

Fig. 4a   **Fig. 4b**

Fig. 4c   **Fig.4d**

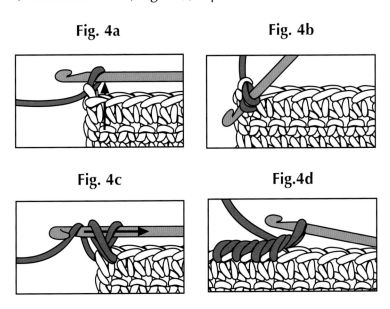

We have made every effort to ensure that these instructions are accurate and complete. We cannot, however, be responsible for human error, typographical mistakes, or variations in individual work.

YARN INFORMATION

Each design in this leaflet was made using Lion Brand®
Cotton-Ease® medium weight yarn. Any medium
weight cotton yarn may be used. It is best to refer
to the yardage/meters when determining how many
balls or skeins to purchase. Remember, to arrive at the
finished size, it is the GAUGE/TENSION that is most
important, not the brand of yarn.

For your convenience, listed below are the specific
colors used to create out photography models.

#1 Tackle it with a Twist!
#148 Turquoise

#2 Extra Elbow Grease!
#100 Snow

#3 Grime Buster!
MC - #194 Lime
Color A - #148 Turquoise
Color B - #100 Snow

#4 Lots of Suds!
MC - #194 Lime
CC - #100 Snow

#5 Put Your Heart into It!
#191 Violet

#6 Real Men Do Dishes!
#112 Berry

#7 Finished with a Flourish!
#099 Almond

#8 Nine Rounds and
You're Done!
Color A - #099 Almond
Color B - #125 Hazelnut
Color C - #186 Maize

#9 One Red-Hot Scrubber
MC - #195 Azalea
Color A - #099 Almond
Color B - #186 Maize